ANIMAL ASSASSINS

by

DAVID TAYLOR

Discover the deadly facts
of the animal world

ANIMAL ASSASSINS

by

DAVID TAYLOR

Discover the deadly facts
of the animal world

D. Quinn

Introduction

Animal assassins – the name isn't quite right. Certainly many kinds of beast *do* kill with the stealth, cunning and total lack of emotion that were the hallmarks of the original assassins – a band of secret murderers founded by Hassan-i-Sabbah in Persia at the end of the eleventh century, who carried out their killing under the influence of the drug hashish (hence their name). No, the term 'assassin', murderer, can be applied correctly only to *one* species of animal among the 2 million or so that live on this earth. Only *man* kills for pleasure or political reasons or out of malice. Other animals kill without emotion. True, killer whales seem sometimes to attack just for fun, and the same might be said about the way foxes can savage a hen-house, biting off the heads of the birds without feeding on most or any of them. Sudden murderous 'civil wars' have been recorded in recent years in chimpanzee society, and our imperfect knowledge of animal behaviour cannot explain the causes. Cases of killing babies, parents and leaders occur in animal species other than man, but often logical social, territorial or safety reasons lie behind the killing.

Animals can be divided roughly into two groups: those that kill other creatures to feed and survive and those that don't. This book is concerned with the first group – the predators, the hunters, the killers. By tooth, claw, poison and suffocation, and with the aid of amazing equipment that is far more advanced than anything possessed by the army, navy or air-force, these animals, some small, some large, some in the sea, others on land or in the air, go efficiently about their business.

Photos on pp. 7 (R.I.M. Campbell), 8 (J. Visser), 9 (C.B. Frith, Michael Fogden), 11 (Gunter Ziesler), 14 (Jack Dermid, Leonard Lee Rue), 17, 21 (Gunter Ziesler), 24 (Norman Myers), 25 (Rod Williams), 27 (Michael Freeman), 30 (Neville Coleman), 38 (J. and D. Bartlett), 39 (Ken Balcomb), 44 (Jane Burton), 45 (K. Wilmshurst), courtesy of Bruce Coleman Ltd; photos on pp. 35 (V. and R. Taylor) and 38 (P. Morris), courtesy of Ardea London; photo on p. 34 (Flip Schulke) courtesy of Seaphot Ltd; drawing on p. 30, courtesy of Mary Evans Picture Library.

First published in Great Britain in 1987
by Boxtree Limited

Text copyright © 1987 by David Taylor

ISBN 1 85283 006 9

ISBN 1 85283 013 1 Pbk

Illustrations by David Quinn
Designed by Grahame Dudley
Typeset by York House Ltd, London
Printed in Italy by New Interlitho S.p.A.-Milan

for Boxtree Limited, 25, Floral Street,
London WC2E 9DS

Contents

Abbreviations

mm millimetre
cm centimetre
m   metre
km kilometre
ha hectare
gm gram
kg kilogram

The Snake

You have 8 hours to live! And you don't know it. You are exploring the deep Burmese jungle in the hope of photographing gibbons. It has been hard work. You hope it's all going to be worth it as you wipe the sweat from your throat. But the gibbons are proving hard to find!

Haaaa-shsh!

Near your right leg, a snake, dark brown in colour with dull gleaming skin scales, has reared. Its head, small and with dark, unblinking eyes, is almost a metre above the ground, while its neck is held in an elegant swan-like S-shape. The rest of its body, perhaps 4.5 m long, is coiled on the ground. In the centre of the coil you notice a number of off-white eggs – about the size of hens' eggs. You have blundered on the snake's nest. You freeze – but not quickly enough. The enraged snake expands some of its foremost ribs, displaying its terrible

A cobra threatens . . .

hood. You are confronting *Ophiophagus hannah*, the most dangerous of all snakes, the one that is unafraid of man, aggressive when disturbed, strong and equipped with highly dangerous venom – the *king cobra*!

The mouth is half open and you can see the dark red tongue flicker towards you. Your foot moves a fraction. Like the crack of a black whip the cobra strikes forward at your ankle. It feels as if you've been slapped. Not really painful. You stagger back. The cobra does not follow. You stop to inspect your ankle. Two spots of red can be seen on your sock. You pull it down. Blood oozes from a pair of small slit-like wounds. The ankle throbs slightly but there is no pain, no swelling. You have 7 hours and 58 minutes to live!

You must get out of the jungle: you decide to set off without delay.

You can't suck the wounds. You decide against a tourniquet (something tied very tightly round a limb to stop the blood from flowing and keep the poison at bay) – you've got to walk on that leg. You squeeze the ankle, hoping to press some venom out of the wound – the bleeding increases slightly. Sweating more than ever, you set off again. You can feel the ankle but it's not really painful. Perhaps a bit puffier now. Not discoloured.

Almost 2 hours later, you stop. The ankle is definitely puffy now. The bleeding has stopped; you feel very tired and slightly light-headed. The bitten ankle is numb; both legs feel wobbly. You have developed a great thirst, but your appetite has disappeared. You sweat continually and lie back exhausted. One of your eyelids droops and won't be raised – you have 5 hours and 41 minutes to live!

Some time later, you cannot stand up. Your right arm doesn't seem to belong to you. You can barely open your eyes but you don't feel any pain. The world seems to spin in a whirl of colours but you can

Cobras spread their ribs to form a hood

control it – just. You haven't the energy to become panicky. You have 3 hours and 4 minutes to live. Then, the venom of the king cobra, a complex chemical mixture that strikes at the nervous system, will finally stop your heart.

The snake – an animal that throughout the ages has been associated with death, treachery, cunning and evil. But does the snake deserve its reputation as a deadly killer with strange powers? The answer must be yes – and no!

Much that has been said about snakes is untrue. They cannot sting with their forked tongues, hypnotize with their gaze or poison babies through their mother's milk by biting her. But they *do* kill 30,000 to 40,000 people every year (half of these in India).

They can detect what's going on around them by tasting the air with their flicking tongue; they 'hear' through their chest walls; some species can 'see' in the dark by means of infra-red detectors (which pick up light that humans can't see); and they can 'bite' after death! They aren't cold and slimy to touch and they aren't very fast-

Cobras kill 30,000 to 40,000 people each year

moving. 11 km per hour is about the fastest they go on level ground, perhaps 24 km per hour when fleeing downhill. Their strike is not as fast as the snatch of a human hand. The danger comes in not knowing *when* a snake is about to strike.

Snakes, of which there are over 2500 different species, can be found in all parts of the world except the Arctic and Antarctic, New Zealand, Ireland, the Azores and most of Polynesia.

My list of the 10 most dangerous snakes in the world includes the *king corba, mamba, tiger snake, puff adder, death adder, diamondback rattlesnake, Russell's viper, bushmaster, ringhals* and *Indian krait*. Just over 400 kinds of snake are venomous, and over half of these belong to the family *Elapidae*, which contains cobras, coral snakes and kraits.

Snakes are reptiles. Like all reptiles, they are cold-blooded, air-breathing vertebrates (animals with backbones) covered with protective scales. Like most reptiles they lay eggs, from which their young emerge. The distinctive features of the reptiles which we call snakes are elongated bodies and lack of legs, though traces of hind limbs can be found in some species, showing that millions of years ago they walked on all fours. Snakes move by wriggling from side to side (not up and down, like caterpillars).

The eye is protected by a transparent sheet of skin which is sloughed off with the rest of the skin from time to time so that the animal can grow. Sight is good, but a snake only pays attention to moving objects. The snake hears by feeling vibrations in the ground through its long chest and jawbones. The sense of smell is well developed, but the snake's most important sense-organ is its tongue, which picks up scent molecules in the air, brings them back into the mouth and touches them against a special organ in the roof of the mouth.

The delicate sensations are then transmitted via nerves to the brain for analysis. This 'smell-taste' function enables the snake to detect the slightest changes in its surroundings.

Snakes are carnivorous. Some species, such as the European *grass snake*, eat their prey alive, while others first kill it by poison or squeezing. The bones supporting the lower jaw can move in such a way that the snake can swallow prey very much wider than itself. The teeth on one side of the mouth are hooked into the victim; then those on the other side are pushed forward and hooked in. The action is repeated, and in this way the snake literally pulls itself over its food. If two snakes seize hold of opposite ends of the same animal, one of the snakes will end by swallowing the other one as well as the prey! Teeth are often broken off, but by the side of each tooth is a cluster of new teeth. As soon as a tooth is lost, a new one moves into its place. Because the jaw muscles of a snake can work for some time after the creature is dead, killed snakes have been known to bite and even inject venom when carelessly handled.

Venomous snakes use special teeth, fangs, in the upper jaw to inject poison. The venom is actually a poisonous form of saliva. As well as killing prey it also helps to digest it. Some snakes have grooved fangs at the back of the mouth and chew the venom into the wound,

The pretty but deadly Coral snake

while others have a pair of poison-injecting fangs at the front. In some species these can fold back, like the blade of a flick-knife.

Snakes with fold-back fangs can carry longer fangs than those without. When the upper jaw is almost at right angles to the lower the deadly fangs swing forwards and downwards into position. Venom passes down a channel from a gland at the top of the fang to a hole close to the point.

The length of the fangs is important, particularly to human beings. Short fangs are easily broken and often fail to inject when striking. Long-fanged snakes, on the other hand, can easily cut through clothing. The longest fangs are those of the *Gaboon viper*, whose fangs can reach over 5 cm long. However, some of the most dangerous snakes in the world (such as cobras and kraits) have fangs that do not fold back.

The venom of snakes is a highly complicated substance that varies from species to species. Because of this it is important to have the right antivenin when treating snake-bite. There are two main types of venom: one attacks the brain and nervous system, while the other works on the blood. Some snakes, such as rattlesnakes, produce venom

The highly venomous Krait

containing both types of poison. The most dangerous venom (as opposed to the most dangerous *snake*) is that produced by sea-snakes living in the Western Pacific and Indian Oceans.

Snake venom is a cloudy, pale-yellow liquid, and is usually only dangerous if injected. But the *spitting cobras* of Africa spit rather than inject their poison, and can aim it accurately over a distance of up to 3 m.

The effects of a venomous snake-bite depend on many factors, such as the type of snake and where you are bitten. Panic and excitement after being bitten increase the danger. One of the most important rules for the treatment of snake-bite victims is to keep them calm, quiet and reassured. In Britain the only venomous snake is the adder, which is hardly one of the most dangerous species: it has killed only 7 people in the last 50 years.

Not all dangerous snakes are venomous. There are others, called *constrictors*, that kill by coiling themselves around their victims and

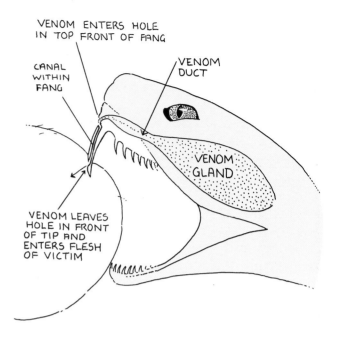

A rattlesnake's bite

A snake can swallow an animal much broader than itself by 'dislocating' its jaws

squeezing them until they suffocate. These snakes are bigger than their venomous relatives – though it is difficult to be accurate about just how long they grow. It is said that boa constrictors 35–6 m long have been killed in South America – but no one has kept skins or skeletons as evidence!

Scientists estimate the length of the biggest constrictor snakes at a lot less than this. The biggest is the *anaconda*, which can reach up to 13 m. Other giants are the *rock python* of Africa and the *reticulated python* of South East Asia (up to 9–10 m), the *amethystine python* of Australia and the Philippines (7–8 m) and the *boa constrictor* of South and Central America (5–6 m). Giant snakes like these can easily kill and devour a human being. But do they?

Although they do not possess venom, constrictor snakes have a powerful and rapid bite. They seize their prey in their jaws and throw a loop or two of their body around it. They do *not* strangle the victim. What happens is that, when the victim breathes in, the snake tightens its coils so that the victim has less room to breathe. When it breathes again, the snake pulls tighter – and so on, until the victim has no more room to breathe and dies of suffocation.

Although anacondas live deep in the jungle, other giant constrictors may live close to people's dwellings. In some areas, pythons and boas are encouraged to make their homes beneath houses to control rats and other rodents. They are highly unlikely to attack man unless cornered and harassed, normally preferring to slip silently away or to stay still and blend into the background. The prey is generally nothing much bigger than an animal the size of a rat or rabbit. Anacondas in the jungle, however, are known to take peccaries (members of the pig family) weighing 40–50 kg, and a rock python almost 5 m long is known to have swallowed an impala antelope weighing 59 kg!

But have they *ever* eaten humans? The answer is yes. In 1927 a Burmese jeweller sheltered under a tree during a thunderstorm and was killed and eaten (feet first!) by a python about 8 m long. In Burma in 1972 an eight-year-old boy was gulped down by a python; relatives of the boy later killed and ate the snake in revenge. In 1973 in Mozambique, a python devoured a young soldier. The victim's body was later recovered from the snake's stomach.

Certainly the big constrictor snakes are easily powerful enough to overcome and kill a man. Even the ones that are only 3 or 4 m long can be dangerous if their coils pin your arms to your sides and then squeeze the arteries in your neck. Working alone with constrictor snakes is consequently something I try to avoid. It proved fatal to a solo circus performer who allowed a coil of a reticulated python to encircle his neck. When he collapsed, blue in the face, people thought it was all part of the act – until it was too late.

A rock python devours a gazelle

The Spider

*I*magine that you are a Californian mouse. You live in a warm, dry comfortable nest beneath the floorboards of a small wooden hut – a hole in bone-dry soil that is littered with crisp brown leaves – along with your family. Usually you spend most of the daylight hours napping and only go outside at night when the hawks have stopped hunting. But today, as the others sleep, you clamber up through a hole in the floorboard and squat on your hind legs looking and listening intently. No sign of human, dog or cat. No strange noise. No unfamiliar smell. The coast seems clear. But it isn't. You don't realize it, but your left hind paw is resting on a fine silver thread, so fragile that you cannot feel it against your skin – yet by touching it you have set off an alarm. A small glistening black individual about the size of a pea, with a bright red hour-glass emblazoned on her underbelly, receives the signal sent along the thread by your paw. She comes hurrying over to investigate.

Almost at the same time you set your forefeet on the floor ready to move off. You hardly feel the prick on your left thigh, but the pain that follows is unbearable. Your whole rear end seems to burst into flame. You lurch forward, but your hind legs refuse to function! The agony blazes and then suddenly vanishes. Darkness. Although your legs

12

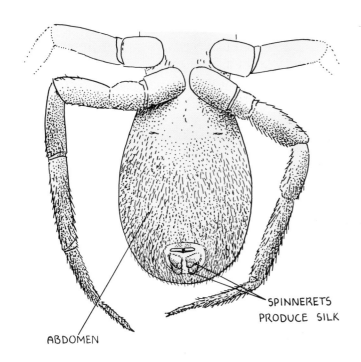

ABDOMEN

SPINNERETS
PRODUCE SILK

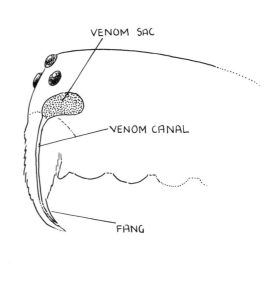

VENOM SAC

VENOM CANAL

FANG

twitch weakly, you know nothing about them. Your brain has stopped functioning – for ever. The *black widow spider* perched on your thigh begins calmly to suck the first juices from your dead body.

Spiders are *not* insects but members of a group of animals called *Arachnids*, which includes scorpions, ticks and lice. Arachnids have 8 legs (not 6 like insects) attached to a body that is divided into 2 parts – the head and chest, and the abdomen. Spiders, of which there are around 40,000 species, are different from other Arachnids, and all other animals, in having 'spinnerets' on their abdomen, which pump out liquid silk produced by glands within the body. On contact with the air the silk solidifies into a strong thread. Not all spiders make webs or snares. Most use their silk for other purposes, such as spinning egg cocoons and lining burrows.

Nearly all spiders have poison glands; the poison is injected into the victim through an opening near the tips of the fangs. All spiders are carnivores. They kill their prey by inflicting a wound with their fangs, injecting a special substance

Above left, the rear end of a spider; right, the front end

that liquefies the tissues, and then sucking out the fluid.

Many kinds of spider spin silk to catch their prey. Some make webs: several types of web design can be found, each more or less typical of a whole spider family.

All web spiders live in a world of touch, and the web serves not only as a snare but also as a telegraph system. The male *garden spider* literally 'telephones' his chosen bride. He attaches a thread to her web, which he plucks in a certain rhythm. The vibrations that the female sends out in her turn tell the male if he is in danger of being eaten, or whether he can risk mating.

Spiders don't have it all their own way; even the biggest and most fearsome-looking ones have enemies. Many lizards, some toads and various birds that feed on insects also eat spiders. The large marine toad has been seen greedily gobbling down hairy tarantula spiders!

13

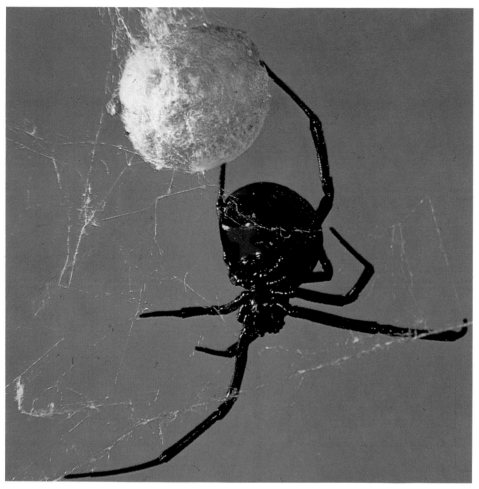

A female black widow guardi her egg sac

A bird-eating spider, below left

The biggest spiders in the world are the *bird-eating spiders* of South America, which are often wrongly referred to as 'tarantulas'. They are

hairy, thick-legged animals that can reach 10 cm across with legs spread, and weight up to 85 gm. They sometimes stow away in shipments of bananas and always give the dockers or greengrocers who discover them a fright. In fact, they are *not* dangerous to human beings. They can give a painful bite if they are upset, but their venom is not a real threat to large apes such as you and me. Bird-eating spiders normally prey by night on insects, but they do from time to time kill bigger creatures.

The *tarantula* is a smaller spider that occurs in southern Europe and that has been known since Roman times to be poisonous (the name comes from the Italian town of Taranto). Its bite kills insects at once and can kill a large mole in about 36 hours. In a human being the bite produces pain and fever but is unlikely to kill.

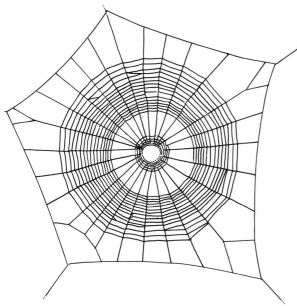

Two different spider web designs, above and below

But are there spiders which can seriously poison and perhaps kill human beings? Yes, there are. Probably the most venomous spider in the world is the female *black widow* of the United States and the West Indies. This creature produces a venom that is 15 times more powerful than that of a rattlesnake. It killed at least 55 people between the years 1726 and 1943. Luckily nowadays an antidote (antivenin) is available.

A country-lover, the *black widow* is frequently found in places where there are likely to be plenty of insect visitors. The males are small and harmless to man, but the female is bigger with a glistening black abdomen bearing a bright red mark. This is easily seen, as she usually hangs upside-down from her tangled web. Although by nature shy, the female black widow attacks at once if her web is disturbed. The poor male black widow knows he risks being eaten by his spouse when he goes courting, so first he 'rings her up' by sending signals down threads to her web. If her reply is polite, he approaches. As a precaution, he loosely binds her with silken strings before mating. Once this is over the female breaks free and the male tries to clear off before she makes a snack of

him. The eggs are laid in round white cocoons of silk. After about one month, the spiderlings bite their way out. They have to fend for themselves at once – otherwise they will eat one another and Mum often gobbles up some of her brood! To humans the bite of the black widow can be painful. Intense pain and cramps follow. Black-widow venom mainly attacks the nervous system, and 4 per cent of all human victims die.

Other dangerous spiders are the *brown recluse* or *fiddleback spider* of the United States and Australia, the *funnel-web spider* of Australia, the *button spider* of South Africa, the *flax spider* of Argentina and the *jockey* or *red-backed spider* of Arabia and Australasia. But 99 per cent of all spider species cause humans no harm at all. Even those that can harm us do not go looking for trouble. Spiders are fascinating and useful animals. They destroy nothing and in no way compete with man for food. What's more, they control insect pests on our behalf. And, remember, they greatly outnumber us – it has been calculated that in the English countryside there are about 2.25 million spiders per acre!

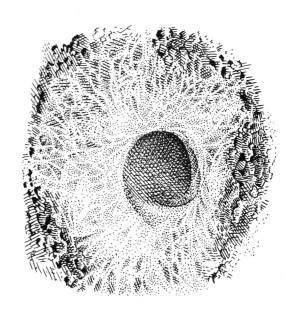

The Tiger

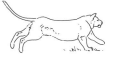

Imagine you are a sambar – a graceful Asiatic deer – standing by the river's edge. The water moves slowly by. Around you some of your family and friends are drinking delicately. All of you have your senses on red alert.

Large ears search the air for the first sound of danger. Big eyes scan the scene, while the muzzle sucks up the refreshing water as quickly as possible. Nostrils analyse the air blowing off the river for unusual odours. You pick up a whiff of wild pig, some rotting vegetation.

Nothing threatening – yet. Coming down for water is essential but hazardous. You don't become an adult sambar if you're careless at drinking-time! You must keep those athletic legs tensed and ready to go at the blink of an eyelid. Your quick reflexes and running-ability are your only defences.

At the forest's edge, reeds bend rhythmically with the breeze. The light dances on the stems, helping to hide the perfect assassin. He's been there for an hour now and it's doubtful whether you could spot him even if you were a mere sambar-length from his ambush. Utterly silent and still, he is nevertheless totally alert. He positioned himself down-wind of you – his sensitive receptors pick up

An Indian tiger kills a sambar

your cow-like odour, but you have no chance of scenting him. He watches you lower your head for a final swallow. His hind feet make small silent treading movements. His tail twitches as he pulls back on his haunches.

You don't see him emerge from the reeds. The edge of the retina of your left eye is the first to pick up the orange-black flash. By reflex you wheel and leap. Too slow! The assassin launches himself through the air. As his great paws, with claws extended, hurtle into your shoulders and club you off balance, you feel an unimaginably tight squeeze on the back of your neck. Numbness washes over you. Darkness. The attacker, with one expertly judged bite, has dislocated the fourth and fifth cervical vertebrae in your neck, shattering the great nerve called the spinal cord. As the rest of the sambar crash into the safety of the forest, the adult male Bengal tiger gives a short roar of victory. Saliva begins to run in his mouth in anticipation of his first full belly in 7 days.

For me the tiger, not the lion, is the 'Lord of the Jungle'. Stronger, more dangerous, more cunning than the lion, the tiger is indeed king of all he surveys. The tiger, a lone ranger, is the master of the ambush.

Tigers are big cats, one of the 7 species of large relatives of your fireside tabby in the family of animals that scientists call *Felidae* and which includes, with the small wild cats, a total of 35 wonderful cat species.

The first true cats arrived 12 million years ago. 6 million years later, the world was full of cats: lions, lynx and giant cheetahs roamed the forests of Europe, Asia and China. Half a million years ago, cave lions and leopards had spread throughout Europe, giant tigers were found in China, and giant jaguars padded across North America. Gradually, the great family of cats colonized every land-mass except for the polar regions, Australasia and some small islands.

Today tigers are to be found in eastern Siberia, Manchuria, Korea, China, Burma, India, Nepal, Indo-China, Malaysia and Indonesia and are everywhere an endangered species. Only a few years ago, 8 sub-species of tiger were alive on this planet. Now we have only the *Indian* or *Bengal tiger* (perhaps about 3000 remaining), the *Indo-Chinese* (numbers unknown but certainly small), the *Siberian* (about 200 in the wild), the *Sumatran* (numbers very low) and the *Javan* (a mere handful – possibly as low as three). The smallest tiger, the *Balinese*, has recently become extinct and the same is probably true for the South Chinese and the *Caspian*.

A few white tigers exist; they are generally not true albinos (lacking all body colour) but have faint brownish stripes and pale blue eyes. Even rarer are the blue-grey tigers which have been reported in China.

What *is* a tiger? Like all the cats, including domestic ones, it is a specialized predatory carnivore. It is built to hunt and kill other animals. The backbone is held together mainly by muscles rather than ligaments as in man, thus giving flexibility of the spine. The design of the shoulder-joints allows the forelegs to be turned in almost any direction. This, together with the retractable claws, enables the cat to grab and hold prey with great dexterity. The

At full tilt, tigers can run 35 miles per hour . . .

hind legs are longer than the forelegs, to make jumping easy, and the skull is wide, with a much shorter muzzle than in dogs, to give space and better leverage for the powerful jaw muscles. An average human adult can bite with a pressure of 20–30 kg. A 54-kg crocodile

. . . but leopards are even faster – they can hit 40 mph

was found to clamp down at a pressure of 698 kg when annoyed, but the *tiger* is thought to chomp away at around the 800-kg mark! The teeth are the ultimate assassin's kit, designed to kill, slice and tear flesh; they cannot grind and chew like humans. The killing bite of a tiger is a remarkably precise affair. Like all felines, it tends to use a neck bite. The prey is killed usually by dislocating the vertebrae in the neck.

The distance between the left and right fang teeth of a tiger is the same as the distance between the neck joints of its usual prey – deer and wild pig. There are special nerves linked to these teeth which sense when the points are perfectly positioned.

Tigers have a good sense of smell, but they rely far more on their eyes and ears. Their eyes are perfectly adapted to work well in the dimmest light. Behind the retina (the part of the eye like a camera lens) there is a screen of sparkling crystals that gathers every speck of available light; it is this that makes a tiger's eyes flash fire in the dark. We think that tigers see in colour,

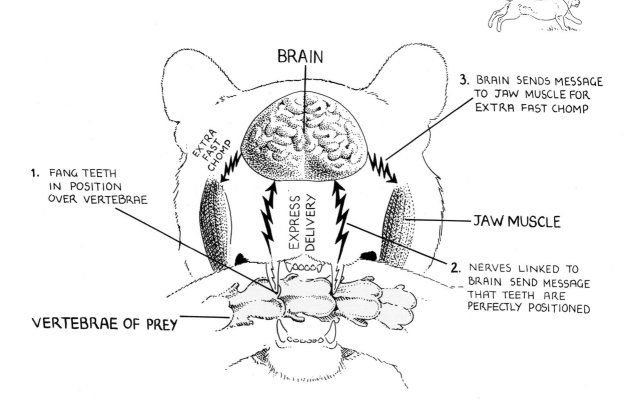

BRAIN

3. BRAIN SENDS MESSAGE TO JAW MUSCLE FOR EXTRA FAST CHOMP

EXTRA FAST CHOMP

1. FANG TEETH IN POSITION OVER VERTEBRAE

EXPRESS DELIVERY

JAW MUSCLE

2. NERVES LINKED TO BRAIN SEND MESSAGE THAT TEETH ARE PERFECTLY POSITIONED

VERTEBRAE OF PREY

The tiger's killer bite

but not very well. Their hearing is much sharper than ours, and with 30 muscles in their ears (as against 6 in man), they can turn their ears precisely to locate sounds.

Like other cats, tigers have whiskers. We do not know exactly how they work, but in the dark they are immensely sensitive antennae, helping the tiger to identify things that it cannot see clearly.

Male Indian tigers are 2.7–3.0 m long from nose to tail-tip and stand about 90 cm high at the shoulder. Their weight is usually between 200 and 240 kg. Siberian tigers are the biggest of all, sometimes measuring almost 4 m long and weighing up to 320 kg.

The most striking thing about a tiger, of course, is its magnificent coat. No two tigers have identical markings, and even the two sides of any one tiger are not exactly the same.

Tigers live in all types of forest, ranging over territories that may be as small as 30 sq km or as large as 4000 sq km. Adults will travel 20–50 km a day, can leap at least 7 m and perhaps sometimes up to 10 m and, being very fond of water, are first-class swimmers who will strike out using the dog paddle

and cover 5 or 6 km easily. They will sometimes attack prey in water and have been known to snatch crew-members from boats anchored in midstream. Although tigers can climb quite well, they don't shin up trees like leopards. They are silent, graceful walkers, moving both feet on the same side together. At full speed, the tiger may reach 35 miles an hour and can cover 4 m in a single bound.

Inside the eye of a tiger

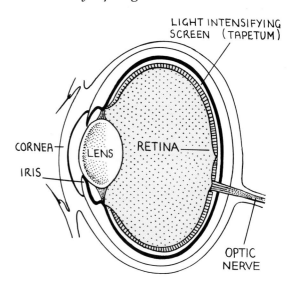

LIGHT INTENSIFYING SCREEN (TAPETUM)

CORNEA

LENS

RETINA

IRIS

OPTIC NERVE

The basic family unit is the female with her young. Animals are ready to breed at 3–4 years of age. 1–6 cubs (usually 2–3) are born after a pregnancy of 103–5 days. Tiger cubs, like domestic kittens, are born blind and don't open their eyelids until they are about 1 week old. The young remain with their mother for about 2 years. Sometimes the families stay together for 3–4 years, but it has also been known for cubs to become fairly independent at the tender age of 11 months.

Tigers prey mainly on deer, wild pigs and antelope, but they will also tackle buffalo, bears, wolves, lynxes, leopards and young elephants.

But, of course, tigers do turn to man-eating from time to time. The most dangerous place in the world for man-eating tigers is the Sundarbans, mangrove swamps of the coast of Bangladesh. Normally tigers are wary of people and try to avoid them, but, when the fleet-footed deer and nimble pigs are too much to cope with, man is a fairly easy target for a disabled or diseased tiger. It is difficult to be sure just how many people have died in tiger attacks, but in India in the years up to 1910 an average of 750 people a year were killed by tigers. Nowadays tigers are much rarer and deaths have dropped sharply, with perhaps 12 persons a year being killed in the Sundarbans.

The tiger is my favourite of all the big cats. Of all the rare and wild animals with which I work, none gives me more of a thrill to see, to touch and, as so often happens, to talk to. Next time you go to a good zoo, visit the tiger and say 'Hello' by making a 'prooch-prooch' noise, rather like a giant purr. Like as not, if he's in a sociable mood, the Lord of the Jungle will answer you back in a most friendly fashion. Fearsome killer he may be, but there isn't a scrap of badness in him!

The snarl of a tiger

The Leopard

*I*magine that you are a Thomson's gazelle – one of the most graceful animals in the world, with a rich fawn coat banded in black, ribbed horns, longish ears, bright, dark eyes and strong, delicate legs. With 50 or so of your fellows, you're moving slowly across an open grassy plain close to the Tanzanian border. The land is dry and the grass is white – it has been a long time since rain fell. Some of you bend necks to nibble as you proceed; others walk with heads high keeping watch and sniffing the air for any hint of lion. To your left, a knot of zebra stand huddled together, their tails flicking constantly.

The assassin, the most accomplished guerrilla fighter in the animal kingdom, the master stalker, wizard of disguise and concealment, sees all these things. All his senses are finely tuned. His weapons are to hand. His instinct, and his years of practice, have made him a killing-machine, more wily than the lion, more vicious than the tiger and more elusive than the cobra. He is the creature whom some of the big-game hunters regard as *the* most dangerous animal on earth – after the great white shark.

His total silence betrays nothing to your nervous ears. Downwind of you, his scent is carried away from your sensitive

Alert for prey

nostrils. Then a blur of yellow and black shadow explodes from the acacia tree, flashes across the grass and merges in a whirling ball of legs, bodies and dust with one of the gazelles. The little victim is dead within 3 seconds of crashing to the ground, its neck dislocated by four precisely placed daggers.

As the herd gallops madly towards the sun, raising a cloud of dust, the assassin takes the body of the gazelle up into the acacia tree and lays it down in a fork of the trunk. The unlucky gazelle, the one nearest to the tree when the leopard attacked, was *you*.

The leopard is one of the most perfectly built cats, strong and agile with a spotted coat that blends easily into the background, particularly in trees. It is an expert climber and a specialized hunter, with sharp sight and hearing and a good sense of smell. It loves to hunt at night, and can identify things in the dark with the help of its highly sensitive long whiskers.

There is one species of leopard (sometimes called the 'panther'), with seven sub-species. The only one of these that is still fairly common is the *North African leopard*, found throughout most of Africa and also in Asia, though its numbers are falling steadily because of persecution by man. The other six sub-species are highly endangered. They are the *South Arabian leopard* of the mountains of Arabia; the *Sinai leopard* of the Sinai desert in Egypt; the *Barbary leopard* of Morocco, Tunisia and Algeria; the *Anatolian leopard*, which is still found in a few places to the south of the Black and Caspian Seas in Asia; the *Amur leopard* of the southern edges of the Soviet Union, Korea and north

Leopards often take their kills upstairs

China; and the probably extinct *Zanzibar leopard*, from the island of Zanzibar, off east Africa.

The background colour of a leopard's coat ranges from pale yellow to almost chestnut. The underparts are white and the backs of the ears are black with white spots in the centre or at the edges which act as 'follow me' signals to leopard cubs. On the shoulders, back, flanks and upper parts of the limbs, the leopard's spots are arranged in rosettes – rings of black enclosing a shaded area, with some having a dark dot in the centre.

Leopards vary in size. The smallest (the so-called 'pigmy leopards') are about 1.8 m from nose to tail-tip when fully grown, while the largest measure about 2.75 m. The average is around 2 m. The weight ranges between 30 and 70 kg.

The leopard is very adaptable and can make its home virtually anywhere where there is enough food. It can be found in all types of forest in Africa, in high and arid mountains, in swampy valleys and rocky deserts, and even above the snow-line. Experts in stealth and camouflage, leopards frequently live very close to human dwellings without being seen. In Africa and India they can actually be found within farms and villages.

Leopards are the best all-round athletes of the animal kingdom. They can run at speeds up to 40 miles per hour. From a crouch on the ground they can leap almost 3.5 m up a tree or cliff, while they can make a long jump of 3 m from a standing position and 6.5 m at full gallop. They usually go up and down trees head-first and are fine swimmers.

Leopards are, as a rule, solitary animals – lone stalkers that rest by day and hunt by night. They tend to go on

24

The black jaguar

Leopards hunt and eat a wide variety of animals – small antelopes and gazelles, baboons, and birds such as storks. Jackals are sometimes taken, as are cheetah, young zebras, pythons, porcupines and hyraxes. Fish frequently form part of the diet, and hungry leopard in Africa have been known to steal catfish from fish eagles. Those that live round villages and farms attack domestic livestock, particularly goats and sheep and less commonly cattle and mules.

The leopard also attacks human beings – and probably always has. Studies of fossils show that early man was a regular ingredient of a leopard's supper!

Some famous assassin leopards have killed over 100 humans. One, the 'Leopard of Rudraprayag' in India, killed at least 125 people before being shot on 2 May 1926. In 1860 another Indian leopard, known as the 'Kahani man-eater', killed over 200 people before being accidentally shot by a man 'who mistook it for a pig'!

The handsome snow leopard

the prowl as the sun is setting, and are not often seen by humans. Groups of 3 or 4 leopards are occasionally seen together. Like tigers, they are territorial animals. Their territories range in size from 8–10 to 21–5 sq km. Typical of cats, the leopard marks its property by scratching trees, scraping the ground, spraying urine and rubbing its body scent onto branches.

Leopards mate in all seasons of the year in Africa and India but only during winter in Siberia. Males often fight for the attention of females. Pregnancy lasts 90–105 days and litters consist of 1–6 (usually 2–3) cubs. The mother alone cares for the cubs, as with tigers, and the newborn animals are kept concealed in a den for the first 6–8 weeks. They are weaned at about 3 months of age. Mother and cubs stay together as a family group until the youngsters are 1½–2 years old. In the wild, leopards live about 12 years (occasionally up to 15), while in zoos they reach 21 or even 25.

The African Wild Dog

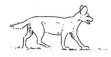

Picture a flat wilderness, with only a few short, spindly trees and tufts of bush. It is silent and still. The air, over 35°C at the moment, makes everything seem to tremble slightly. This is the southern fringe of the mighty Sahara.

At night this arid plain is alive with living creatures. Most of them are underground now – avoiding the fierce heat. But you are an exception – you are a young lion.

Just one year old, you are strong, aggressive and rather inquisitive. You are still with your mother – she continues to teach you the finer arts of hunting. At present she's sleeping. Normally you'd be dozing too.

After a few minutes, you become conscious of a dark shape moving parallel to you. You can't make out what it is. You turn to trot in its direction – a gazelle? The assassin follows you. He picked up your scent 10 minutes ago and he knows what you are.

3 more dark shapes appear. Another appears from behind a bush. You turn your head sharply. You are alert now,

Danger lurks in the distance . . .

Part of a pack of hunting dogs

but hardly frightened. You turn back. The assassins turn too, and move in steadily. You break into a run. They do likewise. They're all round you! Perfectly co-ordinating their courses, the killers approach. Sharp teeth seize your tail. Pained, you spin and lash out. Your claws and teeth are bared. Six more assassins are on you. You throw yourself on to your back, claws raking out. You expel air to produce a last long desperate roar.

The pack of African wild dogs moves in to claim their first meal in 5 days.

African wild dogs are fascinating and skilled predators. They are an endangered species under pressure from human persecution, loss of habitat and disease. Their social life is remarkable and well organized, and they co-operate with one another in a unique way.

The African wild dog is a true dog found only in Africa, from the Sahara down to South Africa. It stands about 75 cm high at the shoulder, with a body 75–100 cm long and a tail measuring 30–40 cm, flared at the end and with a white tip. The coat is short and black-brown, blotched with yellow and white. The muzzle is fairly short and the ears are large.

The species can be found in desert areas, open and wooded grasslands and above the snow-line. The African wild dog belongs to a family of dog-like animals called *Canidae* which hunt in packs. All have some things in common – long, narrow heads with long jaws and plentiful teeth. The cheek teeth are

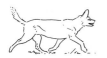

LONG NOSE
LARGE NUMBER OF
SMELL RECEPTORS

An amazing sense of smell

adapted for slicing and grinding and can manage both carnivorous and vegetarian diets. However, the hunting dog eats only meat.

Hunting in the animal world is not just a matter of surprise attacks and quick chases. It is often carried out over long distances; this explains why African wild dogs can kill antelope and sometimes also lone cheetah. An antelope that has bolted off at 60 miles an hour will soon drop to 30 miles an hour or less. This is where the long-distance runners of the dog family come into their own. Hunting dogs will pace one another. When the leaders tire, others move to the front and keep up the relentless pace.

Dogs can see quite well, but most species do not hunt mainly by sight and often overlook creatures that stand perfectly still. Although not totally colour-blind, they see mainly in black, white and shades of grey.

Dogs gobble and swallow rather than chew and savour their food. As you might expect, they have a poor sense of taste. But they have an amazingly keen sense of smell – about 1 million times better than that of human beings! The reason for this marvellous sense of smell lies in the nose. Smell consists of invisible molecules of chemicals floating in the air. When these molecules land on

the special 'olfactory membrane' inside the nose, the nerves carry the information to the brain. In man this membrane covers an area of about 3 sq cm, while in a dog it is almost 130 sq cm, arranged in folds that filter smells from the incoming air. This is why dogs have developed long noses. Even more important, the dog has far more sensory cells than a human. We have 5 million while a hunting dog has around 140 million!

Dogs also have superb hearing. They have large ears with 17 muscles, which allow them to prick up and swivel their ears to pin-point any noise. They can register sounds of 35,000 vibrations per second (compared to 20,000 per second for our ears and 25,000 per second for a cat's) and can shut off their inner ear so as to filter from the general din those sounds on which they want to concentrate.

African wild dogs live in packs of anything from 3 to 30 animals. The usual prey is gazelle and antelope, with an occasional zebra and wart-hog. Although dogs can run at up to 35 miles an hour for long distances, they prefer to pick on weak, lame or young animals. They work together to corner, confuse and finally bring down their victim. There isn't a single predator in Africa that does not try to avoid a confrontation with a pack of hunting dogs.

A pack is composed of both males and females, with one leader of each sex. The two leaders mate once a year. Normally none of the other animals breed. If they do, then the litter of pups will be killed by the leading female.

It is to be hoped that African wild dogs will continue to survive in the wild, and that man will look on them with more compassion and interest in the future, for there may be less than 10,000 left in the whole of Africa.

The Octopus

*I*magine yourself as a lobster – a handsome dark-blue lobster touched here and there with patches of gleaming black.

Home is a small cave. Your fellow lodgers are half a dozen red and green sea anemones that rather brighten up the place, a bunch of small fish who do the cleaning, and an eel that spends most of its time peeping grumpily out of a hole by the cave door.

Today, having dined well on the head of a mullet, you return to the cave just as dawn is breaking. Unknown to you, the cave has a new inhabitant. He moved in while you were out and is now installed on the rocky wall. A little light penetrates the cave, but your dark eyes on their short stalks don't spot him, nor do your antennae sense his presence. He is utterly still, and blends perfectly into his surroundings.

The first thing you feel is a soft 'thunk' as something wraps itself round your left pincer. Almost immediately more soft, supple, immensely muscular bonds are thrown around your trunk and tail. You can't believe how fast they hold you! You try to arch your tail downwards in order to spring back – but you can't. As you rake the water with your left pincer, what seems like a soft blanket is thrown over you. You can't see! A horny beak, strong and sharp, bites down on your back. A stinging sensation shoots along the nerve chain that runs deep along the length of your body. Then – blackness. You have just been killed by a most intelligent assassin, a soft and toothless killer that is a relative of the garden slug. This killer is – the octopus.

The octopus is a mollusc, a member of a great family of soft-bodied animals without backbones. There are around

Pretty but poisonous – the blue-ringed octopus

A giant squid attacks a ship near Teneriffe

45,000 living species of mollusc, and some of them, including the octopus, are grouped together in a special class called *Cephalopods*, which means 'head-foots'. Cephalopods have a longish body covered by a muscular veil of tissue called a 'mantle'. The space between the mantle and the central body-mass contains gills for breathing. Like snails, Cephalopods have a muscular foot that is drawn out at the edges into arms and tentacles. Strictly speaking, octopuses do *not* have tentacles – just arms. In the middle of the foot is a mouth; hence the name 'head-foot'.

Over 150 different kinds of octopus are known to science, though some are very rare. They live only in salt water and many species prefer the most extreme ocean depths. The largest octopus yet discovered is the *giant red Pacific*

octopus (Paroctopus apollyon), which can reach over 9 m across with arms spread and weigh over 100 kg. At the other end of the scale, the smallest octopus is *Octopus arborescens*, which lives off the coast of Sri Lanka. It measures 5 cm across.

Octopuses eat only flesh, feeding mainly on crabs, lobsters and other shellfish. Octopuses are predatory hunters that can shoot through the water propelled by their water-jet, squeeze themselves through any hole big enough to let through their parrot-like beak, and can walk up rocks or over the sea-bed and haul themselves quite quickly across dry land by means of their arms. They can change colour more quickly than the chameleon to blend into the background.

Octopuses can squirt a cloud of ink-like fluid into the water when threatened. The sucker-clad arms have an amazingly powerful grip, but the main weapon is the horny beak. As soon as the octopus bites, venom in the form of specially modified saliva produced by glands opening into the throat is *spat* into the wound, not injected.

Are octopuses dangerous to people sailing, swimming and diving in the ocean? Only rarely, and then under special circumstances. Most of the old reports of giant 'octopuses' attacking men in boats probably refer to large squids.

Fishermen working off the western coast of South America fear the *Humboldt Current squid (Ommastrephes gigas)* more than any other creature living in the sea. But the biggest of all squids is *Architeuthis*, the *giant squid!* Specimens *have* been caught – but no one knows how big they can grow.

The concealed mouth of the octopus

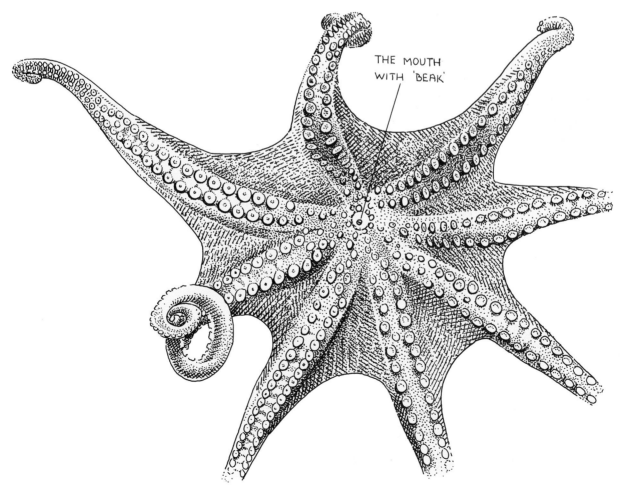

THE MOUTH WITH 'BEAK'

The Shark

You can't believe your luck! Despite everything that the 'experts' told you, there *is* a wreck! The ancient chart, the one everybody said was a worthless forgery, was right after all. 10 m below you, as you hang paddling lazily in the clear emerald water, your heart pounding in anticipation and the clouds of bubbles fizzing upwards in lazy spirals from your breathing-apparatus, lies the skeleton of a ship. Flickering gold and silver shoals of fish wheel about the cannon still jutting from her broken side. An anchor encrusted with coral lies against the underwater cliff that forms the seaward edge of this bit of the Great Barrier Reef off the coast of Australia. No doubt about it – this is the *Vlinder*, an eighteenth-century Dutch fighting-ship that sank carrying a treasure of gold ingots! You make for the wreck.

The kick of your flippers produces a pressure wave which moves out in all directions through the water. Some seconds later this wave, now weak but still clear enough to be picked up by finely tuned detection equipment, arrives at just such a piece of machinery positioned 1 km away. The machine, alerted to your presence, now scans the water with instruments built into it. One of these is a sensor capable of detecting chemical substances in water at a concentration of as little as 1 part per million. This instrument at once identifies molecules of your sweat which

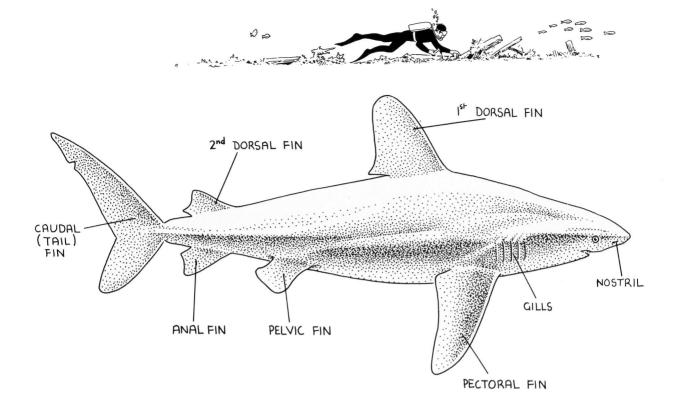

The shark's anatomy

1st DORSAL FIN

2nd DORSAL FIN

CAUDAL
(TAIL)
FIN

NOSTRIL

GILLS

ANAL FIN

PELVIC FIN

PECTORAL FIN

floated away from your body when you became excited at your first sight of the *Vlinder*. At this point, though you don't know it, you become a target.

The machine now starts up its silent-running engine and moves off smoothly in your direction. Probably the most perfect underwater machine ever built glides towards you.

When the machine arrives, you are down on the deck of the *Vlinder* chipping away at a blackened and lime-caked object that might well be an ingot. You don't even catch a glimpse of your attacker before you feel a sickening blow somewhere in the middle of your back. The water turns pink. There is surprisingly little pain. You feel your strength flowing away. You'll not live to bring up your gold. The great white shark, the most deadly assassin in the animal kingdom, opens its jaws for a second lethal bite.

The shark has always had a bad reputation. Few people realize that over the whole of the world the number of humans attacked by sharks in any one year is usually less than 100. Even so,

sharks are the most dangerous family of fish to human beings. Of the 300-odd species of shark known to science, there are many that are harmless to man (including the 2 biggest fish in the world), but 18 species *are* dangerous, and of these the *most* dangerous are the *great white shark, tiger shark, hammerhead shark, mako shark, Ganges River shark* and *white-tipped shark*.

The shark is one of Nature's most successful and long-running designs, one that has changed little in the last 400 million years. Some modern species of shark haven't changed their anatomy for 180 million years. They are ancient fish that literally haven't got a bone in their bodies. Unlike other sorts of fish, their skeleton is made up of a kind of gristle called 'cartilage' rather than true bone.

In size they range from the giant *whale shark*, the largest fish in the world, which can grow to a length of 18 m and weigh up to 40 tonnes, to the tiny *Squaliolus*, which is only 15 cm long and lives in the Gulf of Mexico.

Let us look at a typical fish-hunting

deep-sea shark – a marvel of design and engineering more complex and efficient than any manmade submarine. The basic shape of the shark is streamlined and athletic. A set of fins provides power, stability and steering. The impressive tail fin is the power source. The upper part is bigger than the lower, and, as the shark moves it smoothly from side to side, there is naturally more thrust produced by the top portion of the fin. Part of this thrust is exerted downwards, tending to push the shark not just forwards but also upwards. This balances the natural tendency of the shark's body to sink. The pectoral fins and the flattened undersurface of the shark's body help the shark to steer and rise. The dorsal and the pelvic fins help to keep the shark steady.

The teeth of the shark are nothing more than giant-sized, modified scales, called denticles. The exact shape of the teeth depends upon the species and its preferred diet. Some are long and pointed for grasping prey; some have low blunt crowns for crushing shellfish; some are triangular blades with saw-like edges for cutting flesh.

The bite of a shark can be formidable. Some can easily shear through metal cables, and the force exerted by just *one* tooth of a 2 m shark has been calculated at 60 kg. The power of a shark's bite is increased if it moves in fast, and the shaking of its head and thrashing of its body help it to tear off chunks of food. Sharks have a large J-shaped stomach, which in the larger species is big enough to hold a complete human body.

Sharks can see well the things they need to see, though they cannot discern fine detail. Their eyes are specially adapted to the dim light under water. Like cats they have a shining reflective mirror behind the retina to gather every bit of light and improve eyesight.

The most important sense of the shark is hearing, the ability to pick up and analyse vibrations travelling through water. They are especially sensitive to the sounds produced by the movements of fish or other prey when wounded and struggling.

Sharks have a good sense of smell. The chemicals that carry smell are conveyed through water just as they are through the air, and sharks can follow underwater smells over several kilometres. Sharks have two U-shaped nose-pits or 'nares' – one on each side, between the snout and the mouth. Water continually enters and leaves them, bringing a never-ending supply of chemical molecules for analysis. By comparing the strength of a smell picked up by one nose-pit with the strength of the smell picked up by the other, a shark can tell where the smell is coming from and steer towards it.

Sensitive pits inside the mouth give the shark its sense of taste. If it doesn't like the taste of something, it quickly spits it out.

A diver catches a live hammerhead

Sharks are also sensitive to the electrical impulses produced by the muscles of living creatures and swimming humans, particularly when they move. The electrical sense-organs of the shark are called the 'ampullae of Lorenzini' and are jelly-filled tubes placed in front of the shark's eyes. They may also be used as navigation aids.

The most dangerous shark in the world is the *great white*. This animal reaches about 6 m in length, with a weight approaching 1800 kg. It is found not only in tropical waters but also in the cool temperate zones. Fortunately it is nowhere common. It frequently explores shallow water and even surf. A strong swimmer, it hunts large animals such as seals, sea-lions, dolphins, tuna, sturgeon, turtles and other sharks. In the western North Atlantic it may act as a scavenger, feeding on whale carcasses. It has definitely killed many men and attacked boats.

Why do sharks sometimes attack people? We know that blood and other substances attract sharks, as do certain vibrations produced by movements in the water, particularly those of an animal that is in trouble. Some sharks

The real 'Jaws' – a great white

may attack to defend their territory, and perhaps the short-sighted shark may sometimes mistake a human being for a sea-lion. We are far from understanding all the reasons.

The terrible grin of a great white

The Killer Whale

*I*magine yourself as a ringed seal, plump and sleek, with a handsome coat. You may be awkward on land, but you are a wizard in the water, and now you and your friends are fishing in the cold deep-blue water of the Canadian Arctic. It's winter, with an air temperature this dim, sunless morning of –30°C. The thick layer of blubber beneath your skin keeps you as warm as toast in the bitterly cold water. You dart down 10 m in search of another salmon to round off breakfast.

It's almost black down here. You listen to the rush of water as one of the others swoops up close by and you glimpse a fish-tail sticking out of his mouth. Lucky devil! You use your eyes (which are adapted for use in low light conditions), ears and whiskers to find the salmon you love. There's one! A flick and twist of your hind flippers and you are on him. Snap! One more, and then you really will go up and have a nap.

100 m away the assassin identifies you. He can't see you but he still knows what you are, where you are, your size, your speed and direction of travel. He carries a formidable computer and his long-range ultrasonic detection equipment is far more sophisticated than that of a shark or even a nuclear submarine.

This assassin does not know the

meaning of fear. Why should he? He has no real enemies. He begins to pick up speed. He's almost on you when he emits the first heart-chilling squeal. It's his yell of delight as he goes into battle. You hear the squeal and at once see a darker shadow in the water. A flash of light. Instinctively you spin and shoot upwards, with all your energy forced into your flippers. As you rise, you see a circle of pale white above you. Thank heaven – there's a hole in the ice directly overhead – but the assassin is rising too! One more desperate flail of your flippers and you shoot out on the ice edge. A quick scoot and you are safe. You pause and look at the ice-hole. At once the massive black and white head, jaws gaping, throat red and steaming, pushes up into the howling wind. You lurch hurriedly away across the snow and ice in alarm – you've known of such monsters breaking the edge of the pack ice to get at their prey. When you look back, the killer whale has gone. You've made it this time – *just*!

The killer whale is a member of the family of animals that we call *Cetaceans*.

The family is composed of whales, dolphins and porpoises, but there is no clear difference between them. Killer whales can be thought of either as small whales or as the biggest dolphins!

Cetaceans are mammals, *not* fish. They have warm blood, breathe air, suckle their young on milk and have hair. True, they don't have a lot of hair, but you can see it growing as whiskers round the snout of a baby dolphin or killer whale.

Although killer whales in marinelands are delightful, docile creatures, in the wild they have a reputation for killing anything they come across. It is often said – and I used to believe it when I first swam with big bull killer whales in marinelands or the ocean – that they never attack man, but I no longer believe this.

Reaching a length of up to 7 m and weighing perhaps 4½ tonnes, the killer whale has distinctive shiny black skin and sharp-edged white markings, which

The whale's sonar 'computer'

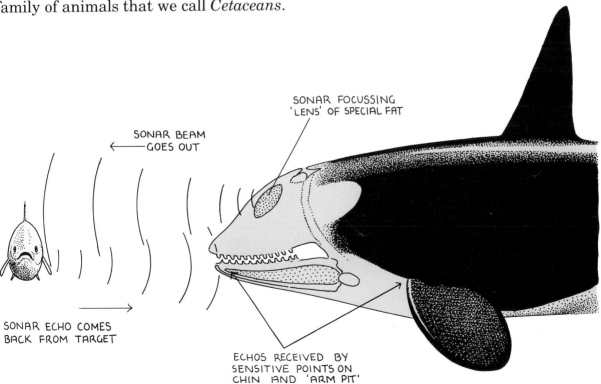

SONAR FOCUSSING
'LENS' OF SPECIAL FAT

SONAR BEAM
← GOES OUT

SONAR ECHO COMES
BACK FROM TARGET

ECHOS RECEIVED BY
SENSITIVE POINTS ON
CHIN AND 'ARM PIT'

Killer whales close in-shore

sometimes been seen to swim into the open mouths of their larger relatives to bite off a chunk of the poor giant's tongue!

Two killer whales will swim one on each side of a gentle Beluga whale and press in on their victim, crushing its chest. Bigger groups of killer whales often work together at herding shoals of fish such as salmon. Sometimes killer whales will tip up small ice-floes, pitching the seals resting on them into the water.

The powerful tail of the whale works by moving up and down. It is the *upstroke* that provides all the forward thrust. As a mechanical device, this tail has been found to be much more efficient than the propeller of a ship.

Killer whales can stay under water for perhaps as long as 20 minutes, while bigger whales such as the *sperm* and *blue whales* can remain submerged for almost two hours. First, they can store

help members of the species to recognize each other. Killer whales are the only Cetaceans that prey upon warm-blooded animals. As well as fish (they adore salmon), they take lots of squid, dolphins, porpoises, seals and sea-lions, walruses, and sea birds such as penguins. They also attack the much bigger baleen whales, and have

The gentle white beluga whale

A killer whale jumps for joy

oxygen, because they have extra amounts of the red blood pigment called 'haemoglobin' and a similar pigment in their muscles. Secondly, they produce energy by chemical reactions in their body-cells that do not need oxygen *in the short term*. They make up the oxygen they need when they surface.

Killer whales can dive deeper than any other whales except the *sperm* and *bottlenosed whales*. They have been known to descend over 1000 m. Unlike humans, they dive with virtually empty lungs and allow their chests to collapse onto their lungs to make a solid lump of tissue.

Like dolphins, killer whales use sonar, ultrasonic beams, to explore the often black world of water in which they live. The beams are sent out as bleeps of varying pitch and frequency. The bleeps bounce back, telling the whale what they are, how far away, and so on. The returning beam is picked up at special points on the tip of the whale's chin and on the armpits (!) and is channelled to the ears within the skull.

Whales and dolphins use sound to communicate with their own species. Their language is complex and has never been deciphered by scientists, despite thousands of hours' work on computers.

Killer whales usually live in groups called 'pods', of 5–50 whales. They can be found in all oceans and seem to prefer colder waters. They do not migrate, but may follow prey for long distances on their own migration routes.

Killer whales may live for 75, perhaps 100, years and reach adulthood at around 9 years for females and 15 years for males. Pregnancy lasts 15 months, and the babies – charming creatures that are *yellow* and black at first – stay with their mothers for several years after weaning, which occurs at 1–1½ years of age.

The Cone Shell

Y ou can't believe it! You are on holiday in Hawaii, looking at the deep-blue sea. Warm wind comes in off the ocean and teases the palms lining the beach. You walk along the sand letting the surf bubble over your toes. Bliss!

Pretty seashells lie on the beach. Your toe catches one as you walk and it flicks out of the water onto the dry sand. It is a beautiful specimen – about 6 cm long and cone-shaped, with an intricate pattern decorating a creamy background. You stoop to pick it up.

Ouch! Something pricks you. You put the shell in your pocket and look at your hand. There is a tiny puncture-point in the middle of what looks like a shallow scrape-mark. There must have been a sharp spine on the edge of the shell. Then the pain begins. Frowning, you walk back to the hotel. Your legs feel weak and the pain is making you sweat. You slump to your knees. Breathing is difficult – your chest feels bound by steel wires. You try to shout but your voice is too weak. Someone sees you and runs over. Your face is pale, perhaps slightly blue – you lose consciousness.

You don't regain consciousness, and exactly 3 hours and 29 minutes later the powerful cone-shell nerve-poison finally stops your heart.

You pick up a beautiful but deadly assassin

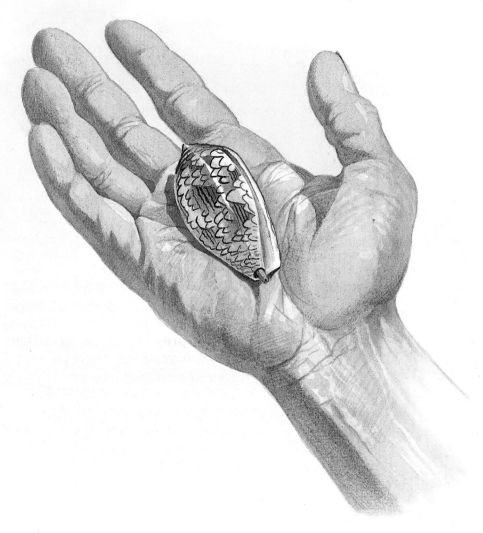

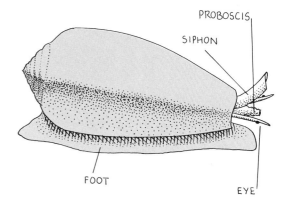

The seashells you are likely to find round European shores are completely harmless. But in other parts of the world – the Indian and Pacific Oceans, for example – there are seashells whose inhabitants are highly dangerous. These are the cone shells, beautiful but deadly.

Seashells are protective houses constructed by snail-like animals. These animals, along with garden snails, are *Gastropods*, part of the mollusc family. There are 30,000 different species of Gastropod, including pond snails and giant African land snails, slugs (who have lost their shells) and cone shells.

A typical Gastropod has a head that can be moved easily and is packed with sense-organs. Behind the head are the internal organs (heart, liver, intestines, and so on), surrounded by a curtain of soft tissue. The upper part of this curtain, the 'mantle', hangs down around the body. The lower part of the mantle forms a muscular foot which contains a mouth equipped with rows of horny teeth (the 'radula'). This curious design, which allows the animal to gnaw at its food with its foot, explains the name Gastropod, which means 'stomach-foot'.

The Gastropod family build spirally wound shells which are always asymmetrical (not the same on both sides). The soft body is also asymmetrical: there are no organs on the left-hand side, and those on the right are arranged in a spiral. As the animal grows, new material is added to the lips of the shell-opening.

Cone shells are distinguished by their lovely shell-patterning and their powerful venom, which is injected into a victim by means of a harpoon-like tooth. There are more than 400 species of cone shell, found mainly in the Pacific and Indian Oceans. Among the most dangerous species are the *tulip cone*, the *textile cone*, the *marbled cone*, the *court cone*, the *striated cone* and the *geographer cone*. Of these, perhaps the

The cone shell and its deadly 'harpoon'

very rare geographer cone is the most dangerous. Some kinds of cone shell have only been found a few times, and I think the rarest must be *Conus dusaveli* – found only once, in the stomach of a fish caught in the Indian Ocean!

The cone shell is really only a sea snail, but one with a remarkable weapon. Deep in the body of the animal is a bag of venom which is connected by a tube to the mouthparts. When the cone shell decides to sting, it pushes a long snout out of its head end. Inside the snout are barbed and hollow harpoon-like teeth (a specialized radula), which are thrust through the victim's skin and inject the venom. Although the cone shell is normally a shy creature, it uses the harpoons as a defence when carelessly handled and to kill prey.

In humans, the effects of the cone shell's sting range from burning and swelling to death within 4–5 hours.

The cone shell is a good example of a humble creature that in its way is as skilled and dangerous as the tiger or wolf.

The Dragonfly

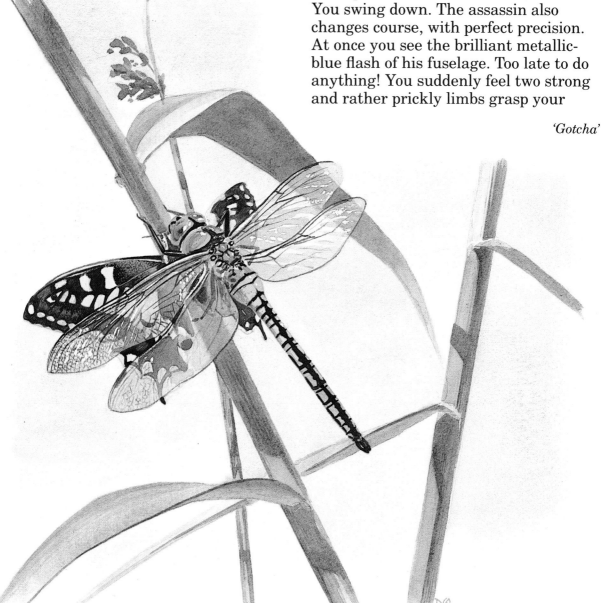

*I*magine it is teatime on a warm July day. The sky is blue, with puffs of cloud overhead; the water of the marshes is like a mirror. A dog barking and the splash of a boat's oars are all that disturb the silence – a backwater fringed with low bushes, reeds and milk-parsley plants.

At this moment you are sitting on a thistle-head. You are one of the rarest and most beautiful butterflies in Great Britain – a swallowtail. Your handsome pair of black and yellow wings carry spur-like points and a pair of red and blue false 'eyes' to confuse predatory birds. Fanning your wings you take to the air. Your antennae tell you that there is some milk parsley just over to the left.

Scramble! Scramble! The assassin, a flying-ace more skilful than the Red Baron, takes off in pursuit of *you*. You don't see him climbing behind you. He has you clearly in his sight – his vision is needle-sharp.

You've almost arrived at the milk parsley, with the assassin steadily closing the distance and still undetected. You swing down. The assassin also changes course, with perfect precision. At once you see the brilliant metallic-blue flash of his fuselage. Too late to do anything! You suddenly feel two strong and rather prickly limbs grasp your

'Gotcha'

42

abdomen. The assassin has caught you! Your fluttering wings seem to have lost all power. The assassin is carrying you through the air. Seconds later he lands on a reed stem, still holding you tight – and then you black out. The dragonfly's two pairs of jaws, armed with crushing and needle teeth, have bitten down hard.

Insects are not the most popular of animals, but almost everybody is dazzled by the beauty of dragonflies. Attractive as they may be, dragonflies are predators that kill and feed on other animals with remarkable efficiency.

Dragonflies are insects, and come in around 2700 different species. They love the sun and are most abundant in the tropics – 500 species make their homes in India and Pakistan. Prehistoric dragonflies included the largest insects that have ever lived. One, whose 300-million-year-old fossil was discovered in France, had a wingspan of 70 cm. The biggest living dragonfly, which comes from Borneo, has a body-length of 10 cm and a wingspan of 19 cm.

Dragonflies have massive jewel-like eyes, two pairs of narrow transparent wings and a very long abdomen, with 6 legs at the front end.

The dragonfly is built as a flying-machine, and as a fighter 'plane rather than a bomber. It lives in the air and some species seldom land from dawn to dusk. Unusually for insects, they can also hover. They are some of the fastest of all flying insects, reaching speeds of perhaps 60 miles an hour. The giant prehistoric dragonfly probably had to fly at least 43 miles an hour just to stay in the air!

To fly so well, the wings of the dragonfly are powered by much longer muscles than are found in other flying insects. The wings are thin but tough, stretched on an elaborate framework of veins. Those species that live in dense vegetation tend to have smaller bodies,

Below, an adult dragonfly's enormous eyes

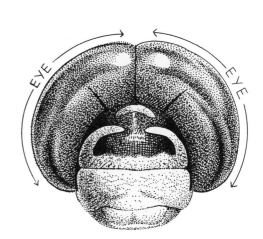

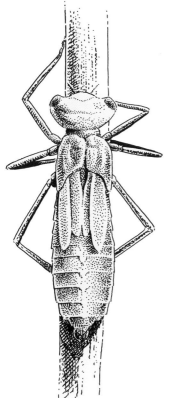

The nymph of a butterfly

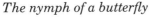

with paddle-like wings better suited to fluttering for short distances between reeds and sedges. To conceal themselves when at rest, they fold their wings against their bodies. Species living around narrow wooded streams, full of obstacles to flight, have broad wings with rounded tips – ideal for stopping suddenly and changing direction. Those dragonflies living by big rivers and unobstructed stretches of water tend to be larger, with stiff, sharp-pointed wings. The most talented aerobatic dragonflies are tropical species, with slender abdomens flattened at the tip to provide a steering-fin! The outline of the ultra-slim body is streamlined, with a head rounded by enormous eyes. The leading edges of the wings are thickened by a series of ridges, and many of the quickest dragonflies lack the microscopic hairs that cover most insects.

The gigantic compound eyes, vital to a dragonfly's hunting-ability, occupy over

A dragonfly nymph kills a young frog

The handsome Emperor dragonfly at rest

half of the head-surface. They give excellent binocular vision, which is important for judging distances, and have over 1000 facets or lenses. These are highly sensitive to movement, and are linked to a sort of computer in the animal's nervous system. At the same time the eyes can see above, below, in front and to the rear of the insect.

There are two main groups of dragonfly. One group have larger, heavier bodies with the hind wings broader at the base than the forewings. At rest they keep their wings stretched out. The other group are slender and both sets of wings have narrow bases. They rest with their wings folded over the body.

Most dragonflies live near water – gnats and mosquitoes are an important part of their diet and their young (nymphs) need fresh water. Adults are highly territorial. Fierce aerial battles often occur, with chunks being bitten off wings. While the slimmer dragonflies mount constant air patrols in search of food and visitors, the plumper types spend more time clinging to reeds by the water's edge, darting out only when necessary.

Dragonflies can mate while flying at full speed. The male recognizes the female by her behaviour and colour. Eggs are deposited in soft plant-tissue just beneath the water-surface by means of the pointed tube (ovipositor) at the end of the female's abdomen. Some species scatter their eggs over the water-surface during flight.

When the eggs hatch, nymph dragonflies emerge. A nymph possesses short wing-pads and a lower lip bearing a pair of hooks which can be shot out to seize prey. The nymph stalks its victims stealthily by walking on its 6 legs, but it can also jet around by sucking water into its back end and then squirting it out again! It breathes by absorbing oxygen in the water around it through gills at the rear of the body.

D. Quinn